A Dance of Dreams

by

Elise Skidmore

Heart Ally Books
Camano Island, Washington

A Dance of Dreams
Illustrations and text copyright © 2015 by Elise Skidmore
All rights reserved, including the right to reproduce this book or portions thereof in any form whatsoever.

Published by:
Heart Ally Books
26910 92nd Ave NW C5-406, Stanwood, WA 98292
Published on Camano Island, WA, USA
www.heartallybooks.com
ISBN-13: (epub) 978-1-63107-008-2
ISBN-13: (paperback) 978-1-63107-007-5

2 3 4 5 6 7 8 9 10 11

Dedicated

To my family,
whose love makes everything possible
&
To my sister, Susan,
who's been sharing my dance since the beginning
I love you.

Contents

Dedicated	iii	The Talking Tree	45
Preface	1	Begin Again	46
Adagio	3	Self-discovery	47
A Dance of Dreams	5	Dancing through the Future	48
Plus One	6	Tell It To Someone Who Cares	49
The Great Oak Tree	7	Settled	50
Heart Bubble	8	Something Old	51
Acknowledgements	9	Walking the Bridge	52
Missing You	10	Peeling Onions	53
Toujours	11	Super Heroes	54
Color Remembered	13	Be Happy Now	55
The Last Time I Was Here	14	The Same, But Different	56
Since You	15	Learning Love	57
March 6th 1947/2009	16	The Damage Done	58
Final Voyage	18	Sweet Craving	61
Self-Portrait	19	The Allure of Egyptian Cotton...	62
Remember Water	20	Elemental	62
Full House	21	Take Time to Appreciate	63
Borrowed Time	22	Forget What I Said	64
Deleted	23	You Can't Take It Back	65
Henry, Still Remembered	25	Always Think	66
Game Over	27	If I Could	67
Growing Old Wasn't Optional	28	She Said/He Said	67
I'll Never Stop	29	Leftovers Of War	68
My Eyesight, the Thing I Miss Most	30	The Poppies	69
Alone In A Room	32	Taken For Granted	70
Before	33	Compulsion	71
The Angel Bus Departs	34	Open Your Eyes	73
That Moment	35	Explaining Tears	74
Beyond	36	Here	77
It's Complicated	37	The Anti-Love Poem	78
Summer Concealed	39	Deus Ex Machina	79
The Persistence of Memory	40	Vegetarian Manners	81
Family Love	41	How To Fill The Glass	82
Ideogram	42	Quarks and the Science of Love	83
Free Choice	43	By The Authority	84

As The Crow Flies	85	*Post, No Bills*	127
Arguing with the Moon	87	*Put Down The Phone*	128
Hold That Thought	88	*Out of Change*	128
Lazy Sunday Thwarted	88	*Two Sides of the Story*	129
The Sea At First Sight	89	*Senyru*	130
Eternity Alone	90	*He Knew Her*	130
In Case Of Emergency	91	*Cast in Stone*	130
Gettysburg	92	*Joy Dances*	131
Johnny's Widow	93	*Rain On Your Parade*	131
Widow's Lament	95	*Texting*	132
Mary	96	*Self-Help*	133
The Man That I Knew	97	*Disappearing*	133
I Shouldn't Be Here	98	*Living With Happiness*	133
Night Write	99	*Local*	133
Jammin'	101	*You Always Come First*	134
Love on a Train	102	*Shelter from the Rain*	134
Complaining About The Weather	103	*Ashes*	136
The Stroke	104	*Timeless*	136
Location	105	*No Words*	136
The Last Straw	106	*Together Again*	137
Too Loud Happiness	107	*Sweet*	138
Springtime Shower In The Park	108	*Yes, Please!*	138
Running With Ice Cream	109	*Inevitable*	138
Doorstep In The Rain	110	*Beached*	139
The Wind	113	*Springtime Ku*	140
I Knew You Were Trouble	114	*Spring Swing Ku Collection*	141
Silent Essay	115	*We Are Family*	143
He Followed The Rules	116	*Cherry Blossoms*	144
Best Kept	119	*Pedant*	144
Occam's Theory of Child-rearing	120	*What matters*	144
Seagulls Lunch At Burger King	121	*(untitled)*	145
Reflections On The Water	122	*Call It A Day*	146
Bury the Evidence	123	*It is Finished*	146
Allegro	125	*Acknowledgements*	147
Automatic	127	*Also By Elise Skidmore*	149
She Wasn't Sure	127		

Preface

Poetry has always held a special place in my heart, even if I don't always understand it. One of my earliest memories is giggling on my father's knee while he recited a German nursery rhyme. The wonderful rhyming whimsy of Dr. Seuss delights me as much today as it did when I was a child.

I remember my mother collecting little poems she liked—in my mind's eye I can still hear her reciting Ogden Nash's Purple Cow and its sequel. Even as a teenager, the lyrics of songs were just as important as the music. When my eighth grade teacher introduced me to T.S. Eliot and Edna St. Vincent Millay (Thank you, Miss Jarmol!), a whole new world of poetry opened for me and I've been wandering through it ever since.

Poetry is Life; it is universal. Like life, poetry can send us on flights of joy and sometimes it can break our hearts. Poets gather the world around them, their own experience and the experience of others, to tell a story, to make us think, to remind us we all share "the human experience". A picture may speak a thousand words, but a poem can create a picture with a few lines. It is reality and imagination combined. It seeks to make sense out of the senseless, and to bring beauty out of ugliness.

This is why I write poetry and take photographs. There is no sweeter sound than to hear someone say, "I know exactly what that's like. I can see this. I've been there." The poems in this book cover a variety of subjects, emotions, and experience. Some I've experienced first hand, others came from creative empathy. It's my hope that you will come away feeling that we have traveled different paths, but we journeyed together on the same road.

Adagio

a succession of slow, fluid movements performed as an exercise in ballet.

A Dance of Dreams

We live in a dance of dreams,
glissade from fantasy
to nightmare
and back again.
Sometimes sweet,
Sometimes bizarre,
Sometimes graceful,
Sometimes with the wobbly legs
of a newborn fawn.
We learn new steps
as we jump to unknown futures
and grow confident in choreography
perfected over time.
Sometimes we dance solo,
other times we revel
in glorious *pas de deux*,
but always we are part of the *corps*.
Life is but a dream we create;
leap into the dance and let yourself soar.

Plus One

I grew up watching coffee perked
in a silver pot with a black handle.
My mother always started with cold tap water.
Savarin was her brand of choice back then;
she measured a scoop per cup into the basket,
plus one for the pot.
As the water inside boiled,
the cover danced and popped,
the glass cap that looked like crystal
bubbled from clear, to tan, to dark chocolate brown,
and the air came alive on the scent
of freshly brewed coffee.

Over the years, the silver pot has been replaced
by a glass electric one, and again
by the automatic drip machine.
Still this sweet memory lives in me,
and I'm told I make a darn good cup of coffee
for someone who doesn't drink it.
I smile to myself and think it's that
plus one for the pot.

The Great Oak Tree

(for Daddy)

Like an oak tree
you stood tall and strong;
you sheltered me from the storm,
and gave of yourself to keep me warm.
You taught me to reach for the sun,
to hear the music of birdsong
and laughter on the wind,
to see beauty everywhere,
especially in the commonplaces.
Like all great oaks,
you were felled too soon.

Heart Bubble

It took a long time
but I get it now.
I understand
the frisson of joy
fizzing in your chest
whenever you see me.
I feel it too.
I am forever
your little heart bubble.

Acknowledgements

I am sorry that I'm not the girl I
used to be, but the years do take their toll
on all of us. And really, on the whole,
I may be overweight but I'm still spry.
I apologize for tears that I cry
too easily; they're not meant to cajole.
In joy or sadness they show you my soul;
I cannot stop them even when I try.
Apologies aside, somethings don't change.
Your face is still the one I long to see
each day. Your smile makes the whole world seem bright;
at whatever cost, it's a fair exchange.
Always by your side is where I will be,
for without you beside me, nothing's right.

Missing You

I see you clearly, waving goodbye
in your sky blue house dress
with the big white polka dots.
Tears run down my cheeks
from the moment the car leaves the curb
and for the next two hours of the drive.
I am inconsolable with homesickness,
no matter that a week in the country
away from the sizzling city heat
is supposed to be fun.
It isn't, even if my aunt does have a big pool
and the ice cream man drives down her street twice a day.
I'd rather run through the sprinkler in the park
and be with my parents.
It's the longest week of my young life.

The day you come to save me from this torture,
I sit on the porch, bouncing with anticipation.
When you arrive, I jump up,
feeling free at long last;
I race to greet you
and throw myself into open arms
that pull me so close
that I'm lost in your ample bosom
in a crushing hug I want to never end.
Happiness overflowing...
No joy can compare to that moment,
no love more heartfelt than a mother's embrace.
No sorrow greater than the impossibility
of it ever happening again.

Toujours

Before we ever met
you were there,
living your life
in parallel to mine,
waiting without knowing
for our lives to intersect.
Once they did,
the beginning was the end
of living separate lives.
Our love is never ending,
and should it happen
that one of us unearths
the undiscovered country first,
they will bide
till we are once again well met.
We live and love,
together
always.

Color Remembered

Though the photo is black and white
there are no shades of gray;
joy sparkles in the little girl's face
as her laughter bubbles forth.

In the picture frame of memory
I can see the red cardigan sweater
that matches the red flowers on the water glass,
the deep green of the potted plants,
and the scrawny fake Christmas tree
with the concrete stand
that my father lugged home on the subway
so my grandmother would have Christmas.

I wonder, does the world ever hold as much color
as when seen through the eyes of a child?

The Last Time I Was Here

The last time I was here
there was an apartment complex,
two stories with Marines
shimmying down the steel beams
that held the building up.

The last time I was here
I was 60 lbs lighter and
35 years younger,
a young bride starting out
in a new place to call home.

The last time I was here
I created memories, happy and sad,
that have lasted through decades of change,
and still I remember the road back
to that long ago beginning.

Now the apartments are gone,
as if they never existed at all;
only the flat skirting remains to mark
what once was the entrance to the parking lot.
Open, empty, and silent,
everything has changed.

Standing in the exact spot
where our one bedroom apartment
with its ugly orange shag rug used to be,
an eerie frisson I cannot describe
envelopes me and lingers.

There is no proof that any of it existed,
except in memory,
and memory can fluctuate.
My husband takes hold of my hand;
we know what is real.

Since You

Since you arrived
drastic changes have occurred;
the world,
the large and the small of it,
will never be the same.

Since you smiled at me
everything I've ever known
exploded into the infinite,
leaving me forever changed—
a new landscape to be cultivated.

Since you captured my heart
I cannot imagine the world
without you in it—
but "cannot" is a lie;
"refuse" is the truth.

Since without you
my world,
and who I am within it,
would be without form and void
as if creation had never occurred.

March 6th 1947/2009

On the saddest day,
the day I became an orphan,
I left the hospice in a daze,
and tried to keep busy
to keep from falling apart.

Thinking of the details
of what needed to be done,
I went to your room
in search of photographs
to create a memorial of
your life well-lived.

The framed photo sat on your dresser
for many long years;
the two of you had eyes for no one
but each other,
and I knew I had to take it with me.
I gently pried open the frame
and was struck dumb.

I stared at my mother's careful handwriting,
words written exactly 62 years to the day before:
Ewald says he loves me and I him.
March 6, 1947

Call it a sign or a message from beyond,
or call it a coincidence if you prefer.
It makes no difference to me;
I know what I know.
You couldn't have said it any clearer.

Final Voyage

You sailed away on uncharted seas
to a place where I could not follow.
Amid tears and forced smiles
we made our farewells
in hope that journey's end would bring joy
and happy reunions with those who
made the voyage before you.
The trip was not planned;
I know it wasn't one you wanted to make,
so I put on my brave face
and promised you everything would be okay.
I kissed you one last goodbye,
then you were gone.
Someday I will board the same ship
to see all the places you've been,
and you will be waving from the shore
to welcome me home.

Self-Portrait

I am the laughing young woman
in the photograph.
Pretty enough, though not a beauty,
thoughtful, kind and full of fun,
who loves to dance and
wishes she drove a red convertible.
She hides her fears and insecurity
beneath a mask of indifference.
Mind over matter—
if she doesn't mind, then it doesn't matter;
if she's not going to get what she longs for,
then she really doesn't want it anyway.

I am still the laughing young woman
in the photograph,
though the mirror says otherwise.
Older, heavier, hair streaked with gray,
but still thoughtful, kind, and full of fun,
even though experience has replaced
much of the carefree abandon
with responsibility and obligation.
Dancing the night away still makes me happy,
and there's a red convertible sports car in my future
if I ever win the lottery.
The mask is crazed,
tenacity filling in the cracks
to keep me moving forward
when innate optimism sags.

Remember Water

I've always been fascinated
by centuries gone by,
loved reading books
and watching movies
of a world where
modern conveniences don't exist.
Absorbed in the life and times
of those long past
I forget the dark realities,
and dream about living in those days.

But then reality intrudes
with common sense,
and I know I wouldn't survive long
if I magically time traveled backward,
for there is nothing
so wonderfully decadent
as stepping into a hot shower
and letting its warmth course over you
for as long as you like,
no convenience as beloved
as indoor plumbing.

Full House

Flipping through photo albums
the world is filled with family and friends.
There is the belly laughter of children,
the off-key tones of "Happy Birthday to you,"
and the too sweet scent of butter cream icing.
There are clinking glasses with toasts of *Gemütlichkeit*,
arms linked in camaraderie as we sway to and fro
to vinyl polkas played on shiny HiFi turntables.
Christmas mornings live, alight with the joy
of childhood wishes come true;
grandparents watch and smile, reliving days gone by
when instead of being happy spectators
all the secret surprises were of their making.
There are little girls with curlers in their hair,
excited and waiting to wear their new dresses
and patent leather shoes on Easter morning.
Colored eggs and chocolate bunnies,
jelly beans and marshmallow Peeps
wait patiently in baskets wrapped in cellophane.
Flipping through photo albums
little ones take their first steps,
and ride their bicycles without training wheels.
Each milestone lives in perpetuity,
as do the family and friends who have moved on.
They are all here, alive and happy,
in a house full of love.

Borrowed Time

I do not understand "borrowed time."
Where do you borrow time and from whom?
Borrowing implies something will be returned,
and time taken cannot not be given back.

I would give much to be able to spend
even a few spare minutes in your company,
but the possibility has long since passed.
I cannot beg, steal or borrow back the time,

But oh, how I wish I could.

Deleted

It's been so long,
I scratched your name from the Christmas card list
and didn't add it to the new address book.
Even though it's been years,
that was hard.

I still see you there,
while scrolling through emails
and my phone contact list.
Even though it's been years,
I can delude myself
that you are only
the push of a button away.

This is silly.
It's been years
and you're never coming back.
In a fit of pique
I end the madness.
Delete.
Delete.
Delete.
Delete.
Delete.
In a burst of technology
you are gone from sight.
I cannot bring you back.

But oh, how I wish my heart had a delete key.

VIETNAM WAR

1959 – 1975

IN MEMORY OF ALL WHO SERVED WITH HONOR AND DIGNITY
THE DIGNITY MEMORIAL® VIETNAM WALL
VA MEDICAL CENTER AT NORTHPORT – OCTOBER 2011
INTREPID SEA, AIR & SPACE MUSEUM – NOVEMBER 2011
CALVERTON NATIONAL CEMETERY – JUNE 2012

Henry, Still Remembered

Long before the internet, email, and social media,
in that long lost era when communication still came
in letters written on paper and penned in ink,
people still made friends with strangers:
We called them pen pals.

In the years before the Summer of Love,
I'd had pen pals from around the world,
young girls my own age and of similar interests.
We shared our cultures and how we wished
we could trade places;
we talked about what teenage girls always talk about—
music and boys.

Henry was different; Henry was a young man.
Henry was a soldier, fighting in Viet Nam.
At first I was delighted to get his address,
excited and a little scared too;
he was only five years older than me,
but at fifteen that felt like eons.
I worried he'd think I was just a kid,
and what could I possibly say that would interest him.

I needn't have worried.
I was too young to realize that talking about normal things
like the weather, music, and our friends,
could be a balm when you're living in a war zone.
Henry was sweet.
He told me about his home in the Midwest.
He never wrote about the war,
and I never asked.

I thought we were getting on well,
even harbored secret fantasies that when he came home
he might stop in New York so we could meet in person,
and who knew what might come of that.

Then the letters stopped.
In the self-centered way of the young
I wondered what I had said or done
to make him stop writing without any explanation.
It never occurred to me
that he might not have been able to write;
in my naivete I never dreamed he might be dead.

I'm ashamed that I didn't consider those things,
that for so long I thought it was about me and my shortcomings.
I was young, but old enough to know better.
I believed in the peace movement;
I had the posters on my walls;
I knew "war is not healthy for children and other living things".
But that's the thing about war—
you don't really know until it touches you firsthand.

Looking back across the decades,
a kaleidoscope of experience changes the view,
blending colors and shading perspective.
I still wonder what happened to Henry.
Did he die in some faraway rice paddy?
Was he taken as a POW, and still among those MIA?
Was he crippled and sent home to recuperate
with more important things to occupy his mind
than writing letters to a teenage girl he never met?
Did he come home broken and battling PTSD?
Did he manage to survive the war to live a full life,
only to suffer the repercussions of exposure to Agent Orange,
the gift that keeps on giving?

I will never know the answers to any of these questions.
The details, like Henry's last name or the state he hailed from, are
    lost to me.
The realist in me knows that these dread imaginings
are not only possible, but probable.

Yet a childlike hope still lives in my heart
that Henry stopped writing because of something that I said,
that he made it home in one piece to live his own happily ever after,
that he lives and loves and laughs there still.

That is how I choose to remember Henry.

Game Over

Coddled, cozened, and coerced,
I played your games
time and time again.
You never cheated,
but you always played to win;
no handicaps given
for age or innocence.

Even when I didn't want to,
I played your games
because I loved you,
because it made you happy.
Sometimes it made me happy too,
even though I rarely won.
Mostly I was glad when
you found new games to play.

All the cards are gone
and the dice have been tossed;
the game boards and playing pieces
were trashed long ago.
Game over.
So why do I long to hear you call,
"Come play with me!"

Growing Old Wasn't Optional

I have become my mother, my father,
my aunts and uncles.
I don't know exactly when it happened,
I certainly didn't choose to become
one of the older generation.
I remember happy occasions
with the family all together,
young, old and in between,
but recently it's hit home
that there is no older generation anymore.
My peers and I are it.
I don't like it much.
I miss knowing there is someone
older and wiser with more experience
I can turn to in time of need,
someone to listen and understand
and tell me everything will all work out.
I wish I had asked more questions
and listened more carefully to the answers;
but the torch has been passed
and I'm not sure I'm up to the task
of lighting the way for future generations.

I'll Never Stop

From the moment when existence
changed from "I" to "We"
loving you has been in my blood.
I'll never stop.
You live within me;
you shape who I am
and the choices I make
that shape who I will become.
I'll never live up to the wondrous potential
you expect from me;
I'll never stop being thankful
that you see the extraordinary in me.
My life is rich because there is "us."
I'll never stop loving you.
Even if the day should come
when I cannot remember the day or the year,
who the president might be, or my own name,
I'll never forget the light you bring to my world.
Look into my eyes and know
the spark still glows in the darkness.
I'll never forget you.
I'll never stop loving you.
I'll never stop.

My Eyesight, the Thing I Miss Most

Yeah, sure, we all know it's better
to get older, considering the alternative,
but there's so much that falls to the wayside
as each year passes that it's tough
to be complacent about it.
So many things we took for granted
back in our salad days are lost to us now—

Sleep, for instance.
I used to be able to sleep ten hours
in a row, long and deep;
now between bouts of insomnia
and having to get up to pee,
I'm lucky to make four.

And then there's memory.
What was I going to say?
Oh, yeah, that's right,
now I remember.

Why is it I can remember
what I wore on the first day of kindergarten
in vivid detail (a brown plaid dress
with white Buster Brown collar
and a wide belt, if you care to know),
the names of every teacher I had
through my elementary school years
(and quite a few beyond that!)
or the name of an actor
who died forty years ago,
and yet I can't remember why
I walked into the room
or the name of the movie
we watched the night before?

And let's not even mention
the aches and pains
that seem to come from nowhere.

But if I had to put my finger
on the one thing I miss the most,
it would have to be my eyesight.
They tell me it's perfectly normal
to need reading glasses
as you get older.
On again, off again, and
where did I leave them.
I don't care if it's normal,
it's a pain in the ass.

I think the Almighty should've
thought this one out a little better.
If we have to slowly become farsighted,
then our arms should slowly grow longer
as compensation.

Alone In A Room

She lies in silent aloneness;
no one really knows if she's aware
of those who wander in and out
to check her blood pressure and other vital signs.
Outside the holiday season blares
with its gaudy vibrancy and rampant consumerism,
but no one really believes she's aware
that it's Christmas,
even though her daughter brought a tree
decorated with red bows to keep on her nightstand.
On Christmas eve her family comes with gifts.
Her eyes for once are open and aware.
"Oh my," she whispers, "but I didn't get you anything!"
Her daughter's eyes are moist with joy—
"It's all right, Mama. Daddy took care of that."
Softly, her husband and daughter sing her favorite carol;
her lips are moving, but they cannot hear the faint words.
They aren't sure if she's singing along or
admonishing her husband to stop his off-key singing
as she has done for half a century.
When they leave, it is the first time in weeks
they have felt she was truly with them,
that they weren't alone,
and they are happy with this rare gift
from the woman they both love so dearly.

Before

Before you made me laugh
resistance wasn't difficult.
Before your smile crinkled your cheeks,
resistance wasn't even an issue.

Before the sweet warmth of your gaze
covered me like melted chocolate,
all the old insecurities had no trouble
keeping secret longings at bay.

Before you cupped my face in your hands
as we shared our first kiss under starry skies,
there was a chance I might have been able
to resist loving you.

After, it was impossible.

The Angel Bus Departs

Goodbyes are never easy;
    endings by their nature are always sad,
    unlike beginnings which hold promise
    and the hope of bright futures.
    Beginnings and endings are inextricably linked;
    each finish is the precursor of a new start.
With tear-stained cheeks I watched
    as you boarded the Angel bus.
    One journey had ended,
    a new one was beginning.
    I knew you would be greeted
    by long lost family and friends;
    I told you to kiss them for me.
    I told you I'd be fine without you.
That was only a half-truth;
    a random song or turn of phrase,
    and you are standing right beside me.
    You are never far from my thoughts;
    missing you is a constant dull ache.
Someday I, too, will step on that bus.
    Until then, I will cherish your farewell gift,
    a boundless, unconditional love that lives eternal.

That Moment

As I watched the sun rise over the clouds
from the top of a volcano,
a new day burst upon the world
in a sea of shimmering white and gold;
I gasped in awe, transfixed.

It was not unlike the sound you made
when you breathed your last breath.

Beyond

Beyond the world that we can see
exists another bright plain.
Beyond the world that we can see,
lives beauty through eternity;
our loved ones we will meet again.
There is no sadness, loss or pain
beyond the world that we can see.

It's Complicated

It's complicated,
this web of tangled emotions
we call love.
So many different kinds,
so many shapes and shades,
shifting in Gordian knots,
impossible to untie
with any grace.
Something sharp is required,
something to make a clean cut,
though it's rarely clean enough,
and too often requires
repeated washing
in salty tears.

Summer Concealed

Summer is not dead.
Concealed beneath fallen leaves
of autumn she sleeps
deep in the long cold winter.
Snow blanket insulation
nurtures and revives
bulbs and seedlings that need rest
in order to thrive.
Everything has its season;
rainbows exist though unseen.

The Persistence of Memory

Wandering through this desert world,
so hot the clocks are melting,
I stretch out my tongue to drink in time.
The precious moments of life
revive this dehydrated soul.
The persistence of memory,
the good, the bad, the happy, the sad,
lifts my eyes to the mountain horizon;
its snowy peaks give me strength
to rise and walk on.

Family Love

Mother's love is first
Before all others she knows
two hearts inside

Father waits with pride
to hold his child in his arms
The world fills with dreams

Open arms reach out
for safety in this big world
Mom and Dad are there

New sibling arrives
that you didn't really want
but the bond grows strong

Aunts, uncles, cousins,
grandparents and greats too,
surround us with love

Ideogram

The ideogram is where it's @.
Words and emotions
have been eclipsed
by symbols, smilies, & acronyms.
Pity the poor wretch,
old-fashioned to the end,
who still maintains
that spelling and grammar
are important
and real words have meaning.

Free Choice

It's always your choice
You are

free to laugh
free to brood

free to give
free to take

free to be amiable
free to be angry

free to focus on the positive
free to see only the worst case

free to learn from your mistakes
free to forever repeat them

free to accept responsibility for your choices
free to lay blame and be the eternal victim

free to open your heart
free to lock yourself away

free to stay
free to go

Choose wisely

The Talking Tree

The tree blinked with
all its animatronic splendor;
its lips moved and spoke to passersby,
who were delighted by this anthropomorphic novelty
even though the conversation was largely one-sided.

My initial reaction was much the same,
but late in the evening when I passed by again,
after the hordes of tourists had scattered
to other more fascinating diversions,
the tree stood still like the inanimate object that it was.

In the empty autumn garden, awash in shades of purple night,
the tree took on the eerie mien of one in an enchanted forest.
Without self-consciousness, I tried to wake him,
to see what secrets he might divulge,
but he must have been too exhausted to speak.
He opened his eyes and blinked: once, twice, three times.
Then without a "goodnight" or "sweet dreams", he went back to sleep.

I wasn't surprised by this lack of interest,
just oddly disappointed that the magic had disappeared.

Begin Again

And so
we shall begin
again, knowing some things
that we did not know the last time.
Hopeful

that we
can get it right,
that we learned our lessons
well and won't make the same mistakes
again.

Endings,
happy or sad,
will always come too fast.
We need to inhale the journey
slowly

if we
want to arrive
at a better place than
where we started on our last try.
Karma

wants us
to do better,
and we must do our part.
Every beginning leads us to
the end.

Self-discovery

Imagine my surprise
to realize that what I once thought
repulsive is now desired above all things
to realize that what I thought I'd never miss
has turned into a gaping hole in my heart
to realize that so many of aspects of myself
are not at all what I thought them to be

Imagine my disappointment
in finding I'd deluded myself for so many years
and in knowing what I crave
depends on the self-discovery of others

Dancing through the Future

The future is subjective.
It could be a minute from now,
a day, a week, a month, a year,
a century or millennium.
Hundreds, thousands, even millions
of choices will be made
with exponential consequences
as humankind's free will expresses itself.
For good or ill, it will be what it will be.
We will live and die and be reborn
in infinite repetitions
as the energy that makes us what we are
shifts and changes in its boundless variations.
And in that limitless shifting dance
we shall live forever,
immortal till the end of time.

Tell It To Someone Who Cares

I'm tired of listening
to the politics of hate,
to the voices shouting
their partisan agendas
without stopping to hear
where common ground
might be reached.

I'm tired of listening
to people bait and bedevil
those whose opinion
differs with their own,
who never take a moment
from their rhetoric to
see where logic fails them.

I'm tired of listening
to those so intent
on pointing out deficiencies
they see in others
that they cannot see their own,
and wonder why
they never learned the Golden Rule.

Instead of listening
to the bombast and balderdash,
I will spend my time
spreading kindness in the world and
bringing laughter to light the darkness.
Let them tell it to someone who cares.
That someone will not be me.

Settled

It's important to remember
that even the most easy-going
can be pushed to their limits.
It may take a while to get there,
but when they reach the critical point
it's the wise man who
slowly backs away until things settle,
else like a bottle of soda
dropped then opened too soon,
you will end up with their ire
exploded in your face.

Something Old

That would be me
feeling like Eliot's Prufrock
pondering the voices
of silent mermaids.
For the time we live in,
the catalog of my years,
while more than middle-aged,
is hardly ancient;
the pages may be worn
but they aren't shriveling to dust.
Not yet anyway.
Experience has taught me
lessons others seem not to have learned,
yet the knowledge leads me nowhere
except to frustration for what I cannot change.
Optimism and Hope are fierce warriors
through the Golden Years,
but I grow weary of the struggle.
Prufrock whispers in my ear:
I grow old.
I grow old.

Walking the Bridge

Walking the bridge
from here to there
seems to take longer
than expected.
We stop midway
to catch our breath,
trying to connect.
The water churns
so far below us;
the buffeting wind
threatens to cast us
into the abyss.
Choices to be made.
Shall we grip the railing
and stand fast
or move forward?
Hand in hand
we forge ahead.

Peeling Onions

Memory peels away in layers,
happiness and sorrow taking turns.
Like slicing an onion,
tears flow freely
and the scent lingers long after
life's stew has been seasoned
and digested.

Super Heroes

Comic strip super heroes don't exist.
You will never look out your window to see
a man faster than a speeding bullet
and more powerful than a locomotive
leaping tall buildings in a single bound;
you will never see a man swinging from spider webs
to stop maniacal villains bent on ruling the world;
or a woman carrying a Lasso of Truth
while flying an invisible plane.
That only happens in the movies.

But real super heroes do exist,
though they tend to walk through the world
largely unnoticed by the masses,
without form fitting costumes,
secret powers, or fancy weaponry.

The mother helping one child with his homework
while nursing another, and wondering
if she'll have time to visit her friend in the hospital.
The father daily fighting a long commute
to a job he hates so that his family
will have a roof over their head and food on the table.
The teacher trying desperately to reach her students
and inspire a love of learning.
The police officers, firefighters, and soldiers
risking their lives for the sake of strangers.

There is nothing extraordinary about super heroes,
and if you asked one they would likely say
they aren't anything special,
they simply act when duty calls.
They battle the everyday with nothing
but tenacity and determination
to do what must be done
in the best way they know how.

Super heroes are all around us.
Look around and see.
You might be surprised to find one
looking back in the mirror.

Be Happy Now

Happiness dithers like you do,
bustling this way and that,
never quite sure when
melancholy will pop up
to scare the joy away.
If you keep looking over your shoulder
trying to outrun sadness,
you will miss all the little joys along the road;
exhaustion will set in and gloom will overtake you.
Then where will you be?

Happiness is a kaleidoscope,
a myriad of color, sizes and shapes,
never exactly the same for any two people.
Whether your exultation comes from
the schadenfreude of your boss
spilling coffee on his khaki slacks,
the music of a baby's belly laugh,
the satisfaction of a job well done,
the bouquet of cognac after dinner,
or the feel of your lover in the dark,
embrace the happiness wherever you find it.

The Same, But Different

We live in a world full of wonders,
populated by the wonder-less,
who do not see marvels
of the universe we live in.
The miracles of life dazzle:
the sun rises and sets,
a child moves inside its mother,
birds and bees and butterflies
dance across a meadow
leaving rainbows of flowers in their wake,
and each lacy snowflake is unique.
In the gray dandelion puffs that cover the lawn
you only see weeds and work;
I see a million wishes blowing in the wind.
We are different people,
who rarely see things in the same way.
You see the concrete and logical,
while I take flights of fancy and
waltz through philosophical dreamscapes.
We are different, yet we are the same,
human beings with the same need
to love and be loved.

Learning Love

He wanted, no, craved,
love to warm his lonely heart;
but no one taught him
to be loved you must give love
without thinking of yourself.

Unconditional,
given fully and freely,
even if it hurts.
The lesson he never learned
no matter how he studied.

The Damage Done

The damage done
is irreparable.

It cannot be undone.

It cannot be mended
or replaced.

A piece of our history
is lost forever;

a piece of my heart
is broken.

What's done is done.

I will not weep;
I will remember.

Sweet Craving

You know the feeling
when you want something
sweet
and just can't escape it
no matter how hard you try

Then you give in to temptation
head out on a quest for that
sweet
yearning that you just can't
get out of your head

That banana split dripping with syrup
or the apple fritter glazed with sugar
sweet
urges drive you hither and yon
until you can think of nothing else

I'm not sure what is worse
Finding what you crave and
binging on an overload of
sweet
that leaves you feeling guilty and sick
or being thwarted at every turn
and settling for a poor substitute
for what you really crave

Either way
sweet
satisfaction
is rarely guaranteed.

The Allure of Egyptian Cotton Sheets

Which has more allure?
Fresh linen on a made bed
or warm rumpled sheets?

Pull back the covers
tucked tight enough to bounce coins
and cocoon yourself,

Or snuggle down deep,
twisted in the heat of dreams,
passions remembered?

Elemental

I am of the water,
you are the air.
When the fire's set,
I rise to meet you.
Molecules intertwine and
we become one.
When the fire cools
we are water and air once more;
but the essence of the one lingers,
sweet and fecund
to perfume the earth.

Take Time to Appreciate

We pay lip service to appreciation.
We make our polite thank yous like mother taught us,
and for that moment we are grateful.
We see a landscape or hear a song
and think how beautiful it is.
Too often that's where it ends;
we move on to the next big thing
without any real thought or appreciation
about how truly amazing the world is.

We need to stop and take stock.
Life is always moving forward;
it doesn't turn around or even slow down.
Revel in every moment for each one is a gift
that comes with a no exchange policy.

Forget What I Said

I wish I'd never said it,
that I could take it back
and wipe the slate clean,
with no trace of the anger
or harsh words left hanging
in the recesses of memory.

But I can't.

No matter how hard I wish it,
words thrown into the universe
exist there forever,
perhaps forgiven,
but never truly forgotten.
Not by you.
Not by me.

But oh, how I wish
I'd never said it.

You Can't Take It Back

I wish you could, but you can't take it back.
It really doesn't matter what you do.
I wish you could, but you can't take it back,
even though your conscience made an attack
on your heart and you know it wasn't true,
a part of me won't ever believe you.
I wish you could, but you can't take it back.

Always Think

Mama said to always
think before you speak;
if you can't say something nice
don't say anything at all.

All too often I bite my tongue,
holding the anger inside,
having one-sided confrontations
in my head until I'm fairly gagging on it.

But it's all retch and no vomit,
it never gets there and spews forth.
The churning goes on in the name of peace,
until I wonder if the silence is worth it.

If I Could

If I could make your problems go away,
I would.

If I could wave a wand or say magic words
to ease your pain,
I would.

If I could erase all your troubles
by taking them on myself,
I would.

I wish I could, but I can't.

But if you could open yourself enough
to share your burden,
I could help you carry the load.

She Said/He Said

She said:
Love this sunny day
with sunglasses and a smile
I hear birds singing
Children playing in the park
run to catch the ice cream man

He said:
The sun is out now
but the weatherman says rain
by the afternoon
The drive home will be a bitch
Idiots can't drive in rain

Leftovers Of War

He had never cared for fish,
and the battlefield cured him
of any affection he may have had
for beans,
but such loathing paled by comparison
to honey.
No remembrance of childhood sweetness lingered;
only the memory
of the honeybees
busily building their hive
in a soldier's corpse.

The Poppies

Poppies blanket the field,
bright red and warm in the sun,
like the blood of those they represent.
Not the thousands of blooms,
nor a thousand times that,
can equal the countless lives spent
over centuries of man's inhumanity to man,
driven by greed, power-lust, conceit
and division over whose invisible god reigns supreme.
Their bones moulder in unknown meadows
and hallowed ground around the globe;
their spirits linger, whispering, "Why?
When will it stop? When will we learn?"
And still the world turns a deaf ear
while the poppies bloom seas of red tears
in hope of remembrance.

Taken For Granted

I take it for granted you're always there;
when morning breaks or when we're deep asleep
in a world of dreams where our demons creep,
I have a safe harbor because you care.

You are the answer to every prayer
whispered to the universe vast and deep.
You are the promise I will always keep—
our souls travel together everywhere.

The world exists because we are in it,
together always even when apart.
You take me for granted as I take you,
like breathing in and out every minute.
We're two people who share a single heart;
without the other nothing can be true.

Compulsion

I must
push on
get it done
I cannot
procrastinate
this time
I will not
fall behind
I must
complete this task
I cannot risk
the consequences
of failure
I must
push on
I must
I must
I must

Open Your Eyes

A famous man once said,
"Living is easy with eyes closed,"
but I cannot imagine
a world of total darkness,
void of the colors of sea and seasons,
where the precious faces of those I love
are fanciful notions concocted
by the touch and feel of familiar territory.

I cannot imagine
standing alone in a strange place
unable to see where I am
or how to get where I'm going
without having a panic attack.
There are things I might adjust to;
books and movies and music
are more easily transformed;
but never seeing the sunrise
or the star-filled universe of the night sky?
I cannot imagine it,
nor do I want to.

I can imagine
that had I never known these things
I might not miss them as much,
that seeing through
touch and sound and smell
might suffice for a good life,
but it's not a life I'd want to endure.
Instead I will open my eyes wide
let the world fill my senses
with all its beauty and ugliness,
and feel blessed to be alive.

Explaining Tears

How can I explain to someone
who keeps a tight rein on his emotions
why my tears so often overflow
for no discernible reason?
I hardly know myself.

While harsh words or anger
can bring on copious weeping,
the fault lies somewhere deep inside me;
it is not wholly the effect of your disdain.
If I could rid myself of whatever causes
those choking, angry tears, I would.

Why the news of the death of someone
I've never met or a sentimental holiday ad
can leave me sobbing, I don't know.
I wish I knew why, sometimes
simply waiting for the traffic light to change
on a sunny afternoon,
I'll feel the swell of tears rising.

I have theories, though none that can be proven.
And none that I could explain
in a way that wouldn't make you feel
helpless and inadequate,
as if it were somehow your fault.

You ask what's wrong
but deep down you really don't want to know;
you are too involved holding back your own demons,
and rather than drowning you beneath
waterfalls of sentimental sadness
I force a smile and say I'm fine.

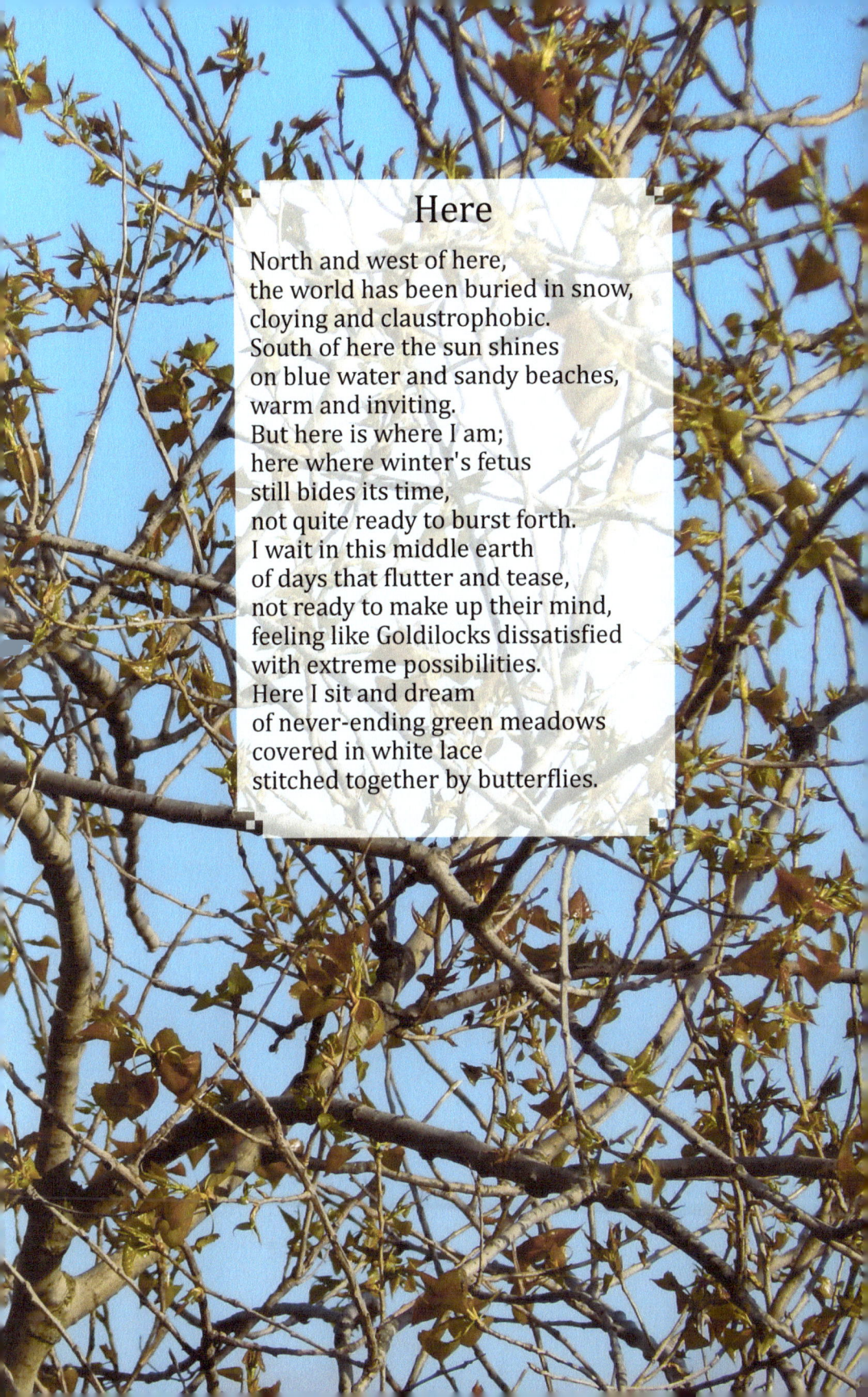

Here

North and west of here,
the world has been buried in snow,
cloying and claustrophobic.
South of here the sun shines
on blue water and sandy beaches,
warm and inviting.
But here is where I am;
here where winter's fetus
still bides its time,
not quite ready to burst forth.
I wait in this middle earth
of days that flutter and tease,
not ready to make up their mind,
feeling like Goldilocks dissatisfied
with extreme possibilities.
Here I sit and dream
of never-ending green meadows
covered in white lace
stitched together by butterflies.

The Anti-Love Poem

Love poems are a bore.
Everything's been said before.
To say "I love you" over and over
soon becomes meaningless rote,
words spoken like a mantra,
an elaborate "Om."

Then again, there are times
I am so angry I want to runaway
screaming at the top of my voice,
when meditation on the "I love you" Om
is the one thing that will bring me peace.

It is an unconscious meditation
that comes without being called.
A tiny unexpected word or deed
born from unspoken "I love yous"
can make the whole world right again.

Deus Ex Machina

Call it what you will,
serendipity, fate, or
the deus ex machina
of some omnipotent someone;
it doesn't matter.
Everything lay in tatters,
the world crumbled at my feet;
then suddenly you were there,
like sunrise at 10,000 feet,
softly exploding into a brand new day.

Vegetarian Manners

I always make sure
I serve non-meat options for
vegetarians,
yet a vegetarian
has never served me a steak.

This seems quite unfair
and a bit discourteous.
And if you ask me,
pasta and a soy burger
will never beat Angus Prime.

How To Fill The Glass

Half empty, you say,
and I fill it to the brim
till it overflows.

That's too much, you say,
and gulp the coffee too fast
without adding milk.

So you burned your tongue.
Bad day ahead, you complained,
should've stayed in bed.

Look at the bright side—
the bad stuff is all done now.
I pour a fresh cup.

Quarks and the Science of Love

Quarks and anti-quarks,
hadrons and atomic mass,
I don't understand.
There are six flavors of quark:
up, down, top, bottom, strange, charm.

High energy hits
produce strange charm—very odd,
from top to bottom.
Is that the science of love?
I felt it when our eyes met.

By The Authority

By the authority given me
from the Universal
High Order of Curmudgeons,
effective immediately:
All pants must be pulled up
so that no undergarments
or nether regions can be seen.
Cell phones and
other technological distractions
are forbidden at meals,
whether taken at home or in restaurants;
diners of all ages will engage
with each other instead.
Addendum—
Any time you are with other humans
you will put the phones away
except in cases of dire emergency.
Also effective immediately:
You will think about who might hear
before you spew bad language.
You will be respectful of others
and remember it's not all about you.
You will treat others as you'd like to be treated.
Failure to comply
will result in excommunication
from the human race.

As The Crow Flies

Not known for its sweet song
like the nightingale or mockingbird,
the crow's squawk is a reminder

of ill omens, harbingers of doom.
Not easy prey for those hunting a tasty meal
like the plump pigeon;
nobody likes eating crow.

Not the prettiest of birds,
certainly no match for peacocks
and their fine plumage
that they can scarcely lift off the ground.

No, I shall go as the crow flies,
fast and fleet,
straight and true,
until I am in your arms again.

Arguing with the Moon

The full Moon's laughter is so bright tonight;
alive with secrets, it dazzles the Sun,
unaccustomed to the competition.
"Tell me, my friend, what brings on such glimmer?"

And the Moon shining brighter answered,
"I find it funny they've got it all wrong."
"Whatever do you mean?" asked the Sun,
puzzled by his lack of understanding.

"They call me a man! How silly is that?
I am female and they should know it well.
Are not their women ruled by my cycles?
My image, their rounded breasts and swollen bellies?"

Indignant because this seemed an attempt
to usurp his omnipotence over
mankind, the Sun burned, shouting angry words.
"Without my light to reflect, you're nothing!"

"You are such a man." The moon shone brighter
with her flirty laugh. "You always think the
world revolves around you. But it doesn't."

"With logic like that you must be female."
The Sun sighed deeply in acknowledgment
that he would never win this argument.

Hold That Thought

"Hold that thought," she says,
and scurries off to help a child
who needs a cookie before he'll give her peace.

I try to stay on the train, I really do.
I grip the handle and hold on tight,
but I'm distracted by a bird out my window.

"I'm back," she chirps brightly in my ear.
"Now what were you saying?"
I haven't got a clue.

Lazy Sunday Thwarted

Motors thrumming
on Sunday morning—
lawn mowers,
weed whackers,
leaf blowers;
alarm clocks set
shortly behind
the early birds
chirping the day awake.
Like those birds
hunting lazy morning worms,
they gobble up sleep
and steal my dreams.

The Sea At First Sight

Raised amid a sea of wheat
as far as the eye could see,
she dreamed of oceans far away.

She imagined blue wheat dancing,
her hair swept back in the wind,
and incessant waves crashing on the shore.

The reality overwhelmed her imagination.

Eternity Alone

The house has more rooms than she remembers;
yet she moves through them with the confidence
born of subconscious familiarity.
Opening doors and turning on lights,
searching for her long lost children,
wondering why they do not answer when she calls.
Again and again,
along dusty hallways,
up and down the stairs,
always looking, never finding her babies.
Systematically searching,
calling their names
over and over;
sometimes calm,
other times angry,
moving on to frantic,
until spent,
she collapses at the bottom of the stairs,
and her mournful wails echo
in the silence.

In Case Of Emergency

Remember to breathe.
That's important.
Your brain needs oxygen
to think clearly.
Remain calm and breathe.

You said it was over,
you couldn't live like this anymore,
then you walked away.
I stood immobile,
watching you go.
I couldn't breathe.
I couldn't think.
Calm was nowhere to be found.

My heart beat in my head,
pounding and insistent.
I raced down the path after you.
Panting, out of breath
and out of mind,
I begged you not to go.

You sighed and with arms wide open
welcomed me into your embrace.
I breathed deep,
inhaled you like air,
and let the calm envelope me.

Photograph by Alexander Gardner, September 19, 1862

Gettysburg

At first glance, just a sleepy little town,
unassuming and pretty to look at,
but bloody history marches through streets and under doors
like an infestation of ants on its way to a picnic.
Minie balls still dot the brick building
where a man worn ragged by the years of sanguinary conflict
penned the speech the world would forever remember.
Three days of war that changed the face of a nation.
Thousands of dead, thousands more mutilated,
an innocent woman shot dead while baking bread—
It looks you in the eye and dares you not to flinch.
The spirits of the dead still wander the long ago battlefield;
in the quiet gloaming you feel them on the breath of a breeze.

Johnny's Widow

It will be over in three weeks you said;
with a heavy heart I prayed you were right.
It's been three years now my dear, and you're dead

with some Yankee musket ball through your head.
My brave cavalier, my bright shining knight—
it will be over in three weeks you said.

Did you picture my face while your life bled
away, as I imagine yours each night?
It's been three years! Oh my dear! You are dead,

never to laugh again, to eat cornbread
with honey, or warm me on a cold night.
It will be over in three weeks you said,

but you were wrong. Damn state's rights and Dred
Scott's head! Forgive my words, so impolite,
but it's been three years, my dear and you're dead—

and when you left we were but newlywed.
You wore gray; I wear black, grief, my heart's plight.
It will be over in three weeks you said.
It's been three years now, my dear, and you're dead.

Widow's Lament

When he's gone you'll know
how anger feels as you're left behind
with no one there who knows you the way he did
with no one there to listen when you turn to share
one of a thousand private jokes
gathered over a lifetime together

When he's gone you'll know
how it feels to be lonely in a crowded room
what it's like to take meals at an empty table
and talk to the place where he used to sit
You'll know how it feels to envy the lucky ones
who don't appreciate how lucky they really are

When he's gone you'll know
how much you miss the snoring you used to complain about
and what it's like to turn in the night
only to be swallowed by the empty space
where your heart used to sleep

Mary

Mary hustles from table to table,
a wily little woman with short blond hair,
taking orders, serving dinner and drinks
to customers young enough to be her grand kids.
She's a fixture at the local Red Lobster;
we marvel that she's still there every time we go.
Always on the move, always smiling,
even in the face of long hours on her feet.

Last time Mary was having an off night,
her usual efficiency deserted her.
Mixed up orders, some totally forgotten,
drinks spilled, not once, but twice.
Apologies overflowed and we brushed them aside—
"It happens," we said. "No worries."

We imagined she wished for retirement,
to not have to deal with the public's demands,
to be able to sit down, relax and be served herself.
It's obvious she takes pride in her work,
as well she should, but time wears us thin sometimes.
She looked like she needed a hug.

When she finally brought the check,
she also brought our forgotten appetizer to go—
"On me," she said, with an exasperated smile,
"It's been a rough night and you've been so patient."

Patience is easy when you see someone's trying their best.
A hug would have been awkward, I'm sure.
We left a large tip instead.

The Man That I Knew

(for Milton)

The man I knew was quiet and kind,
his face etched with the crevices of time,
wrinkles so plentiful and deep
rock climbers could use them as footholds.
The man I knew wore thick horn-rimmed glasses
and had a face that could stop a clock.

And yet as I studied the photos at his memorial,
I saw a man I never knew,
young and handsome, not a wrinkle to be found,
his skin as smooth and luminescent as pearl.
Dressed in his white uniform with Dixie cup hat;
even in the black and white photo, light danced in his eyes,
like he knew the world was his oyster and he only had to open it.

I would not have recognized the man I knew
as the young man in the photograph.
I wondered if Pearl Harbor had wreaked so much havoc
or if that had only been the beginning
of a life with such hardships that could take such a toll.
I wish I'd taken the time to hear his story when I had the chance,
that I'd been close enough to ask the hard questions.

But I never did.
And now I'll never really know
the man that I knew.

I Shouldn't Be Here

I shouldn't be here,
he thought
as he walked through
the tall gates
opened wide and waiting.

I shouldn't be here,
he thought
as he remembered all
the hateful words,
the deceit and the anger.

I shouldn't be here,
he thought
as his eyes filled
to overflowing
with regret and sorrow.

"I am so glad you're here,"
she said,
gathering him in
love's embrace
forever and always.

Night Write

Except for the white noise
of the appliances cycling,
heat pinging through the radiators,
and the stertorous snores
vibrating through closed doors,
the night is silent.

Yet sleep is on the fast track,
miles away and out of sight.
Bathed in the monitor's dim light
she listens to the computer hum
and her fingers tapping at the keys,
wondering if the words will make any sense
when the world awakens
with the coming of day.

Jammin'

Nobody likes being stuck in traffic.
Some may shout and scream and curse,
but not me.
I understand their frustration,
I really do,
especially when things start moving
and there's no visible explanation for the delay.
I prefer that to finding a nasty accident where,
barring a miracle,
you know lives were lost.

I've been slowed down by
dogs in the road,
geese meandering across the street,
and even turtles,
though in the case of the turtles
it was really the good Samaritans
stopping to get them out of harm's way
that caused the backup.
Once, on a trip to Ireland,
we were even held up
by a "sheep jam".
But the strangest traffic jam, by far,
happened when the circus came to town.
Cars backed up for miles,
behind a herd of elephants.

So the next time you're sitting in traffic,
instead of getting angry,
use the time to see what's around you.
Stop and smell the roses—
even if they reek of elephant poop.

Love on a Train

He watched the newlyweds over his paper
while the train rattled along the tracks.
He could tell they were newlyweds by
their shiny new rings and the way they looked
longingly at each other, constantly touching
and stealing kisses that lingered a little too long
(at least for an evening commute on a public train)
as if they couldn't wait till they could tear off their clothes
and tumble into a cloud of rumpled sheets and fat pillows.

He remembered when the world was new
with passion and the promise that love
would always be vibrant and alive like that,
that it would conquer all.
And it did for a time—a good long time,
but no fire can burn that hot for long
without consuming itself.

He sighed at the memory of love's warmth
in the glowing embers,
when passion had burned itself out.
There was comfort in quiet coffee over breakfast,
peace in sitting side-by-side in front of the TV,
contentment at simply being together,
happiness at being two halves of a whole.

Silently, he wished them his same good fortune,
and raised his paper to hide his tears
as the train chugged closer to his empty home.

Complaining About The Weather

If we're very lucky
there might be ten days
out of 365 when
she isn't complaining
about the weather.

It's too hot.
It's so humid.
The wind is blowing the pollen.
It's raining. For days.
They said there might be a hurricane.
It's too cold.
It's going to snow.
They said it'll be a nor'easter.

If she's not complaining
about the weather,
she's complaining about
the effects of the weather.

I'm sick of shoveling.
I hate driving it the snow.
The black ice scares me.
This rain is so depressing,
and the grass is getting so high.
It hasn't rained for days,
now the grass is brown
and the flowers are dying.
My sinuses are killing me.

Sometimes I'd just like to slap her,
but that probably wouldn't shut her up.
There's no point in obsessing
about something you cannot control.
Maybe I'll just sit quietly fantasizing
that a tornado will come along
and carry her away.

The Stroke

It was a stroke,
though not of genius,
that changed his whole world.
In that instant
he was reduced to childhood,
back to basics,
where everything he took for granted
must be relearned.

The words would not come;
he heard them in his head
but they danced away
before he could force them
through lips that refused
to move the way he wanted.

His ungainly shuffle
could hardly be called walking.
Meager steps were an eternity,
guided by spotters
waiting for him to fall.
He hated their solicitude,
but not as much as the cursed wheelchair.
How could something he learned as a babe,
be so impossibly difficult?

He wanted to shout and curse.
He wanted to stomp his feet and march off in a huff.
He wanted to put his fist through the wall.
But his body wouldn't let him
do any of those things.

So he sat where they'd left him
in front of the television,
wishing he had a good book
and fingers that would turn the pages,
while he waited for the next round
of torture to begin.

Location

They say location is everything;
being in the right place at the right time
can make all the difference in the world.
Whether by accident or design,
where we are can change everything.
If you own the last gas station for a hundred miles
or the only restaurant in a small town,
chances are business will be good.
If you have a heart attack when visiting at the hospital,
you're likely to get the help you need without delay.
If you've just finished your manuscript, only to find
yourself on a cross-country flight home,
seated beside a mainstream publisher,
you may have found a helpful captive audience.

You were there when I arrived at the party
I'd only gone to out of obligation.
You rescued me from the jerk with groping hands,
and kept me laughing the rest of the night.
Like a true gentleman, you saw me to my door,
where I invited you in for coffee and you stayed.
You were there.
Now you're here.
Yes, they say location is everything;
that being in the right place at the right time
can make all the difference in the world.
I believe it.

The Last Straw

The last straw.
The short straw.
The one I drew.

Now here I sit
with a dead man,
waiting for help
that will be too late.

Too Loud Happiness

The neighbors invited her to join the party
but Rita always declined.
Their kindness felt like charitable obligation
and their happiness was too loud.
The men exchanging fish stories around the barbeque
reminded her of long ago days
when Charlie grilled the best steaks in town
and had the teeth to chew them.
The children squealing delight as they ran through the sprinkler
only made her ache for her own babies,
who were now grown and gone with babies of their own.
The women tried to be kind;
they offered her tea instead of the wine they drank,
as if it were illegal to drink alcohol after 70.
The truth was she would prefer
a good single malt scotch on the rocks,
and she hated that she couldn't seem to remember
which names went with which faces anymore.
No, their happiness was too loud
and made Rita's head ache so she stayed home.
But a small spark within her
whispered sweet memories
that made her smile.

Springtime Shower In The Park

People in the park
strolling along without care
Yellow flowers bloom
amid the pinks and purples
The world is filled with sunshine

Then suddenly clouds
darken pretty springtime days
rain splatters the ground
an ocean of umbrellas
flee in every direction

The park is empty
except for one little girl
laughing at the rain
Her clothes and shoes are soaked through
still she whirls like a dervish

without care or fear
over what mother will say
Liquid sunshine joy
flying free from every pore
Rejoice in rainbows

Running With Ice Cream

The boy
ran down the street,
ice cream cone in each hand,
soft swirl chocolate and vanilla.
Most odd.

No drips
drench his brown skin.
Whose urgent errand calls?
The ice cream shop is blocks away.
I wonder.

No one
will believe me
when I tell the story.
I wish I'd had my camera
ready.

Doorstep In The Rain

The woman hovers on the doorstep,
hiding from the dreary downpour;
her shoes are soaked and her feet are cold;
she wishes she had the red galoshes
she was forced to wear as a child.

In her pocket there's a folded bit of paper;
she doesn't need to look at it to see
the faded ink on the flimsy yellow page
torn from an old phone book.
She knows the address and number well;
they are etched in her memory though
she hasn't made contact in years.

A car speeds through a puddle;
if not for reflex the splash would have dowsed her
and more than just her feet would be soaked.
Her face is wet, but no one notices
tears in the rain.
She wonders if it will ever stop—
the tears, the rain, the dreary gray
of winter and loss.

Through the blur she sees a man
with a black umbrella that looks
wide enough to shelter the world.
From the instant he stops in front of her,
the world is dry and she feels safe.
He smiles and offers his arm;
she takes it and huddles close.

She crumples the paper in her pocket
into a tiny hard ball.
With no thought of littering,
she tosses it into a puddle
imagining it will follow the runnels
until it flows down the drain,
into the river,
and eventually
out to sea.

The Wind

A gray eyed wolf
encircles the house;
its howling fueled by hunger,
pierces the cracks
and rattles the windows.

Inside I am safe and warm,
curled up in a cozy chair
with a blanket, a book,
and a cup of tea.

No matter how hard he tries,
the wolf cannot blow this house down.

I am safe and warm,
surrounded by sturdy walls,
with a fire in the hearth,
and your arms around me.

And yet
the shrieking of the wolf
still rattles my bones.

I Knew You Were Trouble

Right from the beginning
I knew you were trouble.
You looked like an angel
all wide-eyed and innocent,
but I could see right through
to the devil that lurked within.
After shy introductions
I smiled and we shook hands,
but I knew that you'd leave me
with a mess to clean up.
I knew you wouldn't stay.
I knew you'd break her heart,
but she was so happy,
happier than she'd been for ages—
I couldn't be the one to rain on her parade.
You did that soon enough
and instead of being angry,
she cried and worried about you
when you disappeared without a thought.
Saying I told you so,
that I knew you were trouble from the start,
wasn't going to do any good,
so I held her instead
and wished I'd been wrong.

Silent Essay

Her face is a silent essay of pain
in a language that most cannot read.
The few who attempt to understand
grow weary from the effort to decipher
mixed messages written in code.
They do not see her herculean struggle
to find an eraser to make the pain go away
without turning the paper to shreds.

He Followed The Rules

He followed the rules,
but wondered why
they all seemed
to start with "Don't."

He followed the rules
but wondered why
instead of fitting in,
he always felt apart.

He followed the rules
but wondered why
breaking them
held such fascination.

He followed the rules
because without them
there would be only chaos,
and that just wouldn't do.

He followed the rules,
but oh, how he wanted
to walk on newly washed floors
with muddy shoes,
and not give a damn.

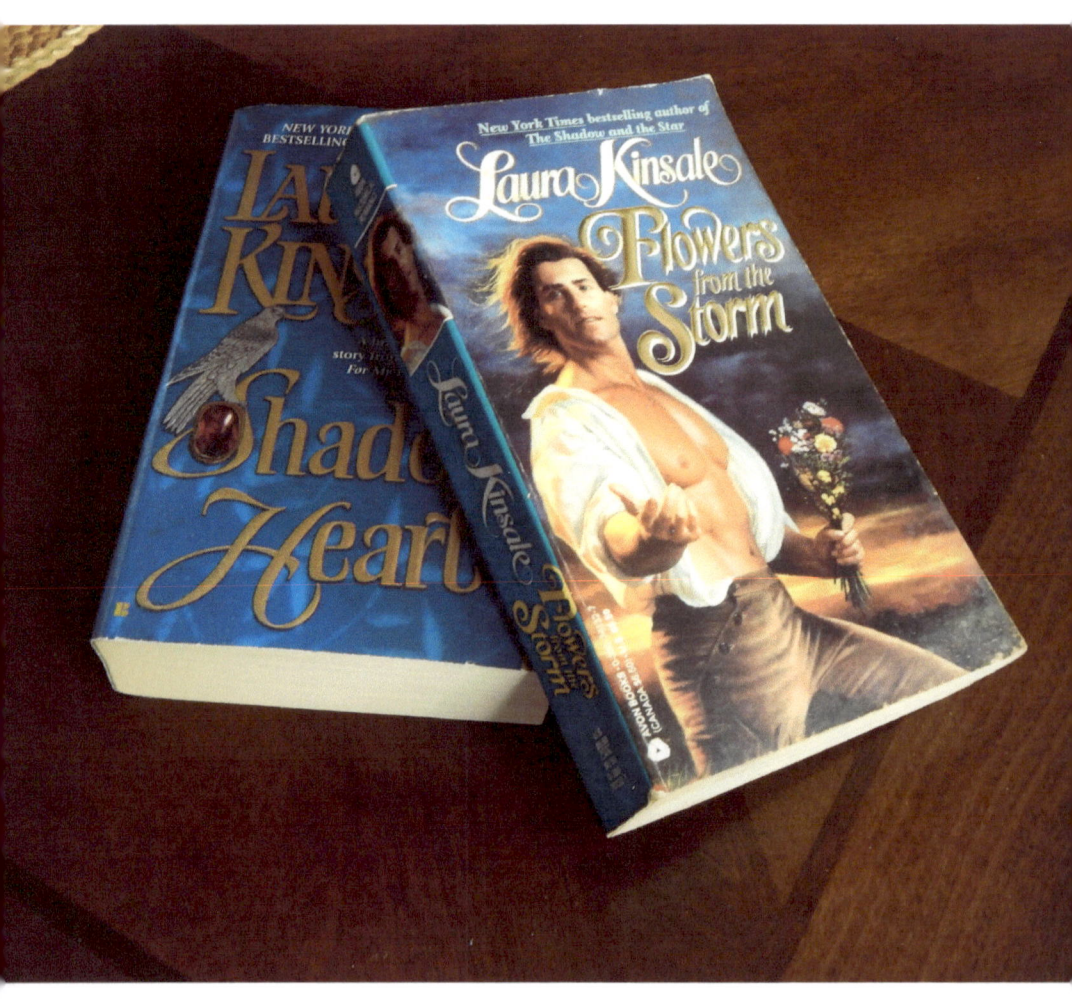

Best Kept

A most eligible bachelor,
for his most substantial assets,
if not for his average stature
and a face that no one
would ever refer to as handsome.

Like everyone else, he has secrets
he guards with utmost care;
he cannot bear the thought
of being pitied or a laughingstock.

Those who know him are used to
seeing his nose buried in a book,
but they rarely ask what he's reading.
When they do he smiles and says,
"Why, the latest bodice-ripper, of course!"
They all laugh, never realizing
he hides his best kept secret in plain sight.

He devours these Romances
like sweet cakes at afternoon tea;
and like the women they are written for,
he enters each story with open arms,
searching for the secret to finding a happy ending.
He imagines himself as the misunderstood hero
who wants to be loved for himself alone;
he wants the intelligent, witty, and passionate woman
to feel for him the way she's never felt about anyone before—
the same way he feels about her.

He wants the happily ever after.
He secretly fears he will never find it.

Occam's Theory of Child-rearing

According to Occam's Razor,
with all things being equal
the simplest explanation is the best.

She scanned the devastation
that had once been her living room,
the upturned coffee table,
the potted plant scattered across the floor,
the family cat hissing from atop the entertainment center,
and popcorn everywhere.

She had been gone less than an hour;
her normally well-behaved son and his best friend
happily playing a video game
while she went to pick up a prescription at the drug store.
What could have happened to incite such riot?

She spotted a large silver bowl she'd never seen before
and wondered where it had come from.
"Oh, that's Zandor's helmet," her son said.
"He was using it for the popcorn,
and I guess he forgot it."

Clearly the boys had gotten into it over something,
though she had no clue what caused the melee.
Why then, as she listened to her son's detailed account
of a hungry alien named Zandor,
who had appeared out of nowhere,
apparently having his signals skewed by sun spots
and needing sustenance before he could go on,
did she almost believe his fantastical story?

Seagulls Lunch At Burger King

Hungry and alone, I ate lunch in my car,
parked in the lot of fast food heaven.
I watched the employees
in their nursery school bright uniforms
struggle to keep a cheery disposition
as they served cars lined up at the drive in window
or battled with seagulls over leftovers, headed to the dumpster.
The gulls were determined and vicious about it;
no one was going to steal their banquet.
Resolute they snatched oil stained paper bags
from overflowing trash cans,
tearing them open inch by inch
till the scraps of uneaten buns, wilted lettuce
and french fries soggy with ketchup
spilled across the asphalt.
Woe be unto the human being
foolish enough to come too near the feeding frenzy.
I couldn't help but wonder
when did seagulls get a taste for Burger King—
and why would they
when the ocean held all manner of fishy delicacies
that is theirs for the taking?

Reflections On The Water

Amid blue skies with billowed clouds
and leaves of dappled green
reflected in the still water,
a young woman daydreams
of futures yet to be.
With the kiss of a summer breeze
lines bloom on her face
as infinity ripples across the pond,
and she weeps for all the lost dreams of yesterday.

Bury the Evidence

"Bury the past," he said.
    "Bury the hate before it eats you alive.
    Can't we just bury the hatchet
    and have peace for a change?"
"I'll bury the hatchet," she said,
    with eyes as cold and dead as winter,
    "In your head."

Allegro

a succession of fast jumps and dynamic movements performed as an exercise in ballet.

Automatic

It's automatic
when I see your smiling face
I don't have a choice
All the world's cares slip away
and I am lost in your eyes

She Wasn't Sure

She wasn't sure
if it was the truth or a lie.
She wasn't sure
if her judgment was good or poor.
But when she looked him in the eye,
somehow she knew she had to try.
She wasn't sure.

Post, No Bills

Down the country lane
rows of rusted mailboxes
wait for the postman.
Open-mouthed and hungry
they hope good news is coming.

Put Down The Phone

Will you look at me?
Forget social media—
Be social with me.

Out of Change

I am out of change.
This machine doesn't take bills.
Chocolate calls my name.
Vandalism is a crime.
Shall I risk handcuffs today?

Two Sides of the Story

Oh happiest day
baby in the family
wonders never cease
New life brings joy to the world
and family continues

Oh saddest day
great grandchild coming
that you'll never know
Your greatest wish will come true
empty arms will not be filled

Senyru

River of tears flows
unnoticed by the masses.
Look close, see them fall.

He Knew Her

Everyone
thought she was a saint
except him.
He knew her
better than she knew herself;
he loved the sinner.

Cast in Stone

Cast in stone,
your opinions are
always there,
unchanging.
Water and time alter rock,
but you never yield.

Joy Dances

Hyacinth,
Honeysuckle, and
hope blooming
together.
Joy dances in the sunshine;
Be one with its song.

Rain On Your Parade

Rain on your parade
cannot dampen your spirit
unless you let it
Splash in the puddles and laugh
Your own sunshine lives inside

Texting

Driving
Full attention
on the phone, not the road
Last important message might be
"OK"

Self-Help

Helping others is
the best way to help yourself
Karma will be kind
Cultivate a giving heart
and your cup will overflow

Disappearing

Our time disappears
gone in the blink of an eye
You are always here
A magician's illusion
No one's really cut in half

Living With Happiness

Our time together
was filled with joy and laughter,
brief but beautiful.
I miss those cherished moments;
they lift my heart daily.

Local

Our journey through life
is often an express train
speeding by too fast.
Let us switch to the local,
pausing to enjoy it all.

You Always Come First

You always come first
I'm at the end of the line
I got the memo

Shelter from the Rain

Sea of umbrellas
bob along the city street
ocean of color
people bumping side to side
scurrying through the raindrops

Ashes

From somewhere unknown
the taste of ashes and smoke
fills my mouth and nose.
Savor unwanted mouthfuls,
the remains of loved ones lost.

Timeless

Mona Lisa smiles
in her eyes the secrets speak
eternal beauty

No Words

I have no words.
Ebola virus scares the world.
I have no words.
Terrorists murder to be heard.
Yet beauty lives in dead leaves hurled
by children dancing in the whorls.
I have no words.

Together Again

We stroll hand in hand;
say "bread and butter," then split
for oncoming trees
and passersby who won't budge,
but nothing parts us for long.

Sweet

Bite ripe strawberries
taste succulent sweet flavor
lick juice from your chin
savor this delicacy
preserved on a lover's kiss

Yes, Please!

Do it again.
Kiss me like you really mean it.
Do it again,
and then again, and ten times ten.
Now's not the time for you to quit,
just when you've got the hang of it.
Do it again.

Inevitable

Inevitable
All good things come to an end,
sometimes bad things too.
Beginnings are happier
but endings can bring us peace.

Beached

waves crash on the beach
undertow covers my feet
dragging me to sea
I raise my face to the wind
where my hair and thoughts fly free

Springtime Ku

amid new green grass
crocuses purple and white
open in the sun

azaleas budding
daffodils bow in the breeze
spring comes creeping in

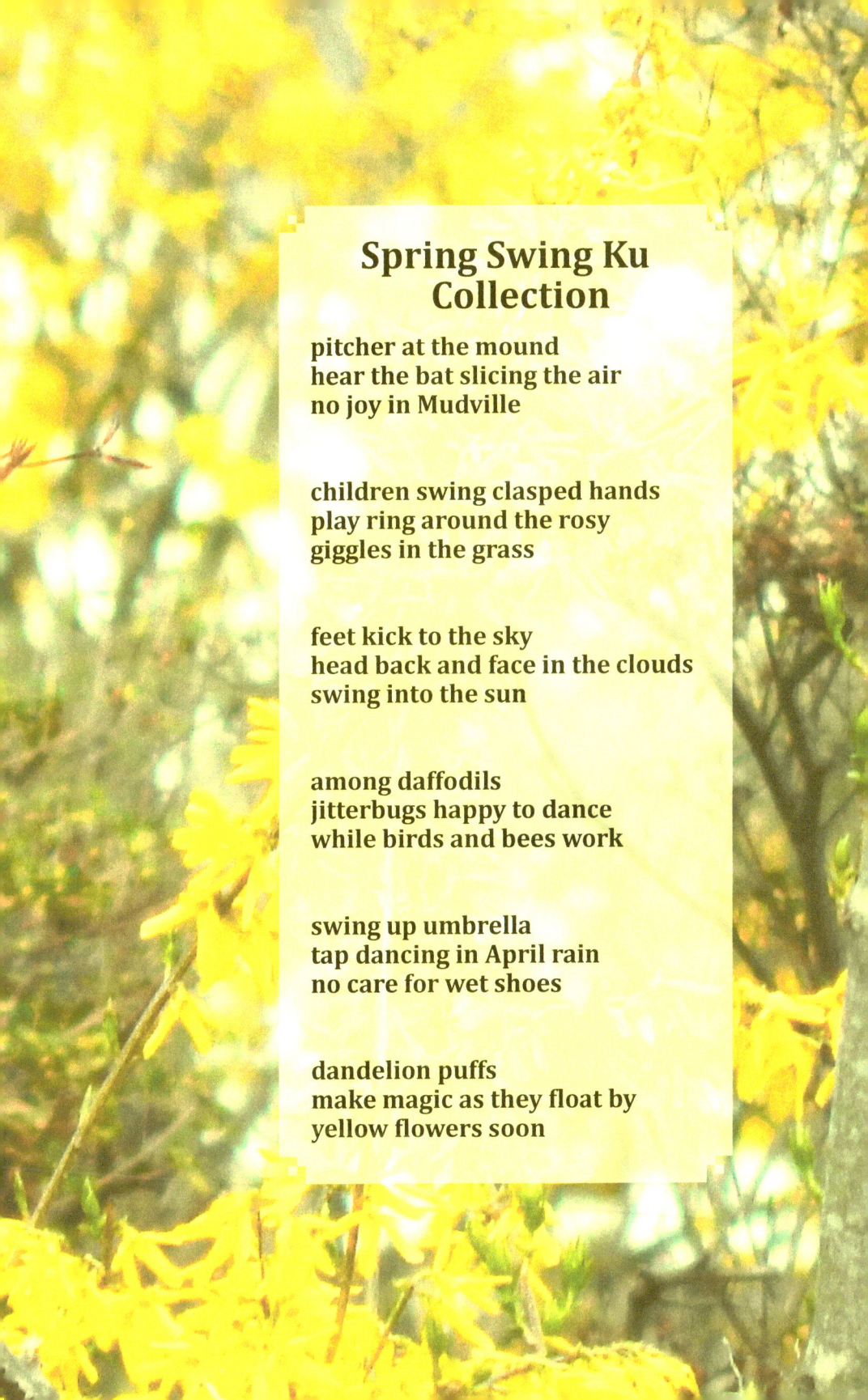

Spring Swing Ku Collection

pitcher at the mound
hear the bat slicing the air
no joy in Mudville

children swing clasped hands
play ring around the rosy
giggles in the grass

feet kick to the sky
head back and face in the clouds
swing into the sun

among daffodils
jitterbugs happy to dance
while birds and bees work

swing up umbrella
tap dancing in April rain
no care for wet shoes

dandelion puffs
make magic as they float by
yellow flowers soon

We Are Family

Each family tree's
roots spread far and intertwine
gnarled fingers hold hands
Side by side the forest grows
create the clan of mankind

Cherry Blossoms

Cherry blossom trees
pink petals soft in the sun
falling in the rain
follow the trail of satin
that leads to serenity

Pedant

I have
been known at times
to nit pick the small things
like grammar and punctuation,
it's true.

Likely
I'll continue
to do so forever.
I cannot seem to help myself.
Oh, well.

What matters

Rude awakening.
You keep apologizing.
It doesn't matter.
You are still alive and whole;
that's all that matters to me.

**One with earth and sea
breathe all encompassing blue
and reach for the sky**

Call It A Day

Last chapter is read
All the characters are well
Time to go to sleep

It is Finished

So it is finished
a passel of poetry
tossed into springtime
with luck they'll take seed and grow
fields of imagination

Acknowledgements

I would like to thank my friend and publisher, Lisa Norman, for her never-ending patience as I struggle with technology, her continued encouragement and support when my confidence lags, and for just getting things done. But mostly, thanks for being a wonderful friend. Without you, there wouldn't have been one book, let alone three.

A big shout out to my long time friend, writing buddy, and CHA sister, Linda Grimes, who's always willing to offer constructive feedback and opinions when I can't seem to make up my mind. Even though she's not a huge poetry fan, she really likes mine, and I love her for that. Plus, she always knows how to make me laugh. And then there's the chocolate.

I would also like to thank my beautiful daughters, Carrianne and Sarah—

Carrianne, for always being willing to read my latest poems and give me honest feedback.
Sarah, for humoring me when I asked her to let me take photos of her down at the beach. Not only did I capture the cover shot for this book, but quite a few other super pictures.

Special thanks to my niece, Nicole Verdi, for allowing me to use one of the photos I took of her youngest daughter, Vanessa. Such a beautiful baby made it difficult to choose just one.

Also By Elise Skidmore

Poems from the Edge of Spring and *When Leaves Fall*

Elise Skidmore's poetry touches on the phases and loves of life, family, friends and the world we find ourselves in. Elise is converting poetry haters into poetry lovers with her accessible poems that delight and entertain.

Ask for Elise's poetry anywhere paperbacks or ebooks are sold.